W9-BHR-632

YOU'VE COME A LONG WAY,
SYBIL MACINTOSH

YOU'VE COME A LONG WAY, SYBIL MACINTOSH

A Book Of Manners and Grooming For Girls

IT WAS EASY —
REALLY NOTHING!

BY CHARLOTTE HERMAN

ILLUSTRATIONS BY TRINA SCHART HYMAN

LAMPLIGHT PUBLISHING

Lamplight Publishing, Inc.
new york, n.y. 10001

Lamplight Publishing, Inc.

Library of Congress Number: 73-2258

ISBN 0–87955–207–7
ISBN 0–87955–807–5 (lib. ed.)

For Paula J. Orellana—
who writes the most beautiful letters
with a fountain pen
and black ink

CONTENTS

INTRODUCTION

You have just been chased away from the dining room table because you happened to spill a whole bowlful of chicken noodle soup in your lap. Your mother says it's all because you spooned your soup in the wrong direction, and if you had any manners it never would have happened. And on top of all that she yelled at you for slurping too loud in front of her important company.

You really can't understand why she's getting so worked up over a little noodle soup. But she's been doing a lot of strange things lately. Like the time her bridge club was over and she kept you hidden in the closet until all the ladies went home. And then there was the time she whisked you into the house through the back door so the delivery man from Sears Roebuck (who came in through the front door) wouldn't see you. And what about the time she introduced you to the Avon Lady as the little girl from across the street, and told the Man from Glad that you were some strange kid selling Girl Scout cookies.

You're not sure why, but for some reason you get the feeling your mother is ashamed of you. Maybe it's got something to do with the way you look and the way you act. Maybe you should wash you face and comb your hair once in a while—even when you're not going to a birthday party. And maybe what you need to learn is a little etiquette. You know what that means. *Etiquette* was a spelling word that you had to look up in the dictionary and use in a sentence. You found out that it has something to do with having manners and being polite. So you wrote, "I have no etiquette."

But now you figure the time has come to do something about yourself—just so you get a little peace and quiet around the house. And as for learning etiquette, who knows? Maybe some of it will rub off on your mother. So instead of turning off the TV in the middle of your favorite program and yelling, "Sybil Macintosh, go to your room and do your homework," maybe she'll just turn off the TV in the middle of your favorite program and say, "Sybil Macintosh, *please* go to your room and do your homework."

Anyway, it's worth a try.

YOU'VE COME A LONG WAY,
SYBIL MACINTOSH

CHAPTER ONE

MANNERS IN GENERAL

The reason manners were invented is because they help people get along with each other. They can even help *you*. Having manners means knowing how to act with people—your parents, friends, teachers, and strangers.

You might even have a few manners you didn't know you had. If you're careful not to hurt anyone's feelings, and if you try to make people feel comfortable when they're with you, you have manners. And because you have manners you wouldn't even think of telling your best friend Marcia that her new shoes are ugly, or telling Marcia's mother that she can't cook as good as your mother can, or saying, "Hi, Irma. Who's your fat friend?"

And because you have manners, you always

say nice things to people when you see them—
like hello, and good-bye, and may I, and thank you
and please. Or do you?

SAYING HELLO

It's nice to say hello to people you know. It's
easier than pretending you don't see them.

Let us suppose you and Marcia are walking
through Woolworth's and you stop at the candy
counter to buy ten cents worth of salted cashew
nuts. Out of the corner of your right eye you spot
your piano teacher, Miss Muldoon, who is walking
toward you. What do you do?

1. Forget the cashews and run.
2. Pretend you're busy looking at the
   chocolate malted milk balls.
3. Look right at her and pretend you
   don't know who she is.
4. Smile and say, "Hello, Miss Muldoon."

If you chose number four, you're right. It's
the polite thing to do. And it's probably the safest
thing to do too. Otherwise Miss Muldoon will wait
until your next piano lesson and call you a snob.
Or she'll tell your mother and you'll get yelled at.
And we already know that manners are supposed
to help people get along with each other. So why
cause trouble? Smile and say, "Hello, Miss Muldoon," and give her a cashew nut.

14

What about saying hello to someone who comes to your house?

"Sybil, someone's at the door. See who it is." (Your mother forgot to say "please.")

"Oh, it's just Mrs. Himmelfarb, Ma."

Saying something like this is front of Mrs. Himmelfarb could bring on a real disaster. You might cause your mother to lose her favorite neighbor. And she's already lost half the ladies on the block because of you. So help your mother by saying, "Hello, Mrs. Himmelfarb. Please come in." Then take your dirty socks and sneakers off the chair, offer her a seat and get your mother.

Or let's say you are expecting Marcia over at any moment because you have to copy a few arithmetic problems from her. The doorbell rings. You open the door and instead of Marcia, you see this pesty little kid, Bruce, from across the street. You glare at him and say, "What do *you* want?" Right? . . . Wrong! You don't say that; not even to a pesty little kid named Bruce. Pesty little kids have feelings too. And besides, his mother is watching from across the street. So you smile and say, "Hello, Bruce," or "Hi, Bruce. No, I can't play with you today. My mother is making me do my homework. Good-bye, Bruce. Be careful when you cross the street and don't talk to any strangers." You say that last sentence extra loud so his mother will hear.

After you get rid of Bruce, you start thinking

15

about Marcia and how she's taking her sweet time getting to your house. When she finally gets there, what do you say?

1. It's about time.
2. What took you so long?
3. I thought you'd never get here.
4. Where's the arithmetic already?
5. None of the above.

Did you get that one? The answer, of course, is *none of the above.* If you do say any of those things, Marcia will probably never let you copy her arithmetic again. So instead, you might say, "Hello, Marcia. It's nice of you to come." Invite her in and *then* you ask, "Where's the arithmetic?"

SAYING GOOD-BYE

You're having the girls over for milk and honey-nut cookies. You're just about ready to eat your fourth cookie when Marcia announces that she has to leave early because she has to go to the dentist.

You don't see any reason why you just can't go right on eating. Marcia's been to your house before. She knows where the door is. Besides, you can't take a chance on leaving the table. There might not be any cookies left by the time you got back. So you keep on stuffing your mouth and wave a little bye-bye to Marcia.

Deep down you have the feeling that this is

not the proper way to say good-bye. So instead, you politely grab a batch of cookies and take them with you as you walk Marcia to the door. You say, "Good-bye, Marcia. Thanks for coming." And if you'd like, you can add, "Have fun at the dentist."

Now let us suppose all the girls are over at Marcia's house. Everybody's eating and drinking and whispering (which, by the way, is not a polite thing to do in front of somebody because it makes a person feel left out of things) so Marcia's mother can't hear.

Some impatient person is outside honking the horn. You know it's your father out there because you can recognize the sound of the horn, and also because he told you he would pick you up at 4:30 sharp and it's now 4:30 sharp.

You make a mad dash for the door because you're in a hurry and because Marcia probably won't even miss you with all those other kids around.

This is another example of rudeness. You shouldn't just disappear from someone's house without saying good-bye first. So you take a few seconds and say, "I have to go now, Marcia. It was fun." And don't forget Marcia's mother. "Good-bye, Mrs. Wertentile. Thanks for the milk and cookies."

SAYING MAY I

It is 11 o'clock in the morning. You're sitting

at your desk in school when suddenly you realize you have to go to the bathroom.

You walk up to Mrs. Fingerhut's desk and say, "Can I go to the bathroom?"

Mrs. Fingerhut says, "May I go to the bathroom?"

You think it's a coincidence that Mrs. Fingerhut has to go to the bathroom at the same time you do. But what you can't understand is why she's asking you for permission. Mrs. Fingerhut doesn't have to ask. She's the teacher. She can go whenever she wants to.

Actually, Mrs. Fingerhut is not asking you for permission to go to the bathroom. She is just correcting your grammar.

Formally speaking (and Mrs. Fingerhut is very formal), there is a difference in the meanings of *may I* and *can I*. When you say *may I* you are asking for permission to go somewhere or do something. When you say *can I* you are asking if you have the ability to do something. So why would you be asking Mrs. Fingerhut if you have the ability to go to the bathroom? How would *she* know? Next time, try saying, "Mrs. Fingerhut, may I go to the bathroom?" (Holding your stomach and having a pained expression on your face might help too.)

SAYING PLEASE

Please is a polite word. It is so polite, you will even see it written on signs.

18

In the park: *Please* don't pick the flowers.

On your neighbor's lawn: *Please* keep off the grass.

On an escalator: *Please* watch your step.

On a box: *Please* open other end.

If signs can say *please* so can you.

Suppose it is 12 o'clock noon, and you and Marcia are eating in the lunchroom. Marcia has brought tons of coconut-covered marshmallows for dessert. You are absolutely wild about coconut-covered marshmallows and are hoping to get at least two. Marcia couldn't possibly eat all those by herself.

If Marcia has any manners, she will say, "Have some coconut-covered marshmallows, Sybil." But Marcia doesn't have any manners, so if you expect to get any, you'll have to do the asking. What do you say?

1. How can you possibly eat all those marshmallows by yourself?
2. Too much coconut in the teeth gives you cavities.
3. Give me one.
4. Oh, I just love coconut-covered marshmallows. Could I please have one?

If you chose number four you're right. It's direct and it's polite.

SAYING THANK YOU

After Marcia gave you the marshmallow, did you just grab it and stuff it in your mouth, or did you say thank you first, and then stuff it in your mouth?

Any time someone gives you something, or does something for you, it's nice to say thank you. You know all that, of course, but did you ever say thank you to your mother for letting you stay up late on a school night, or thank your father when he gave you your allowance? (Or did you just snatch the money and say, "Is that all?") Try saying thank you once in a while and shock your parents.

COMPLIMENTS

How To Give A Compliment

Whenever you think something nice about a person, and you say it, that is called *giving a compliment.*

Your mother has just come home from the beauty shop. You can hardly recognize her. She looks terrific.

"You look terrific, Ma."

You have just paid your mother a compliment.

For a change your mother has made your sunny-side up eggs just the way you like them; hard whites and soft yellows.

"The eggs are delicious, Ma. Just the way I like them."

Another compliment. Maybe your mother will be encouraged to try harder from now on, and you will get hard whites and soft yellows more often. Compliments are easy to give if they are honest.

Watch out for compliments that aren't really compliments at all:

"I'm mad about your new dress, Marcia. You look so much thinner in navy blue." (Marcia is fat.)

"Today your hair looks pretty, Marcia." (On all other days, Marcia's hair looks ugly.)

"Your father was very nice to me today, Marcia." (Marcia's father is usually mean.)

21

How To Receive A Compliment

"Gee, Sybil, what a beautiful sweater. I just love it."

"Oh, this ugly thing? I hate it. I only wore it because my mother made me."

Congratulations. You have just succeeded in making Marcia feel like an absolute fool. She figures there must be something wrong with her for just loving an ugly sweater that you hate.

Next time (if Marcia forgives you and there *is* a next time), try a simple, "Thank you."

TELEPHONE MANNERS

You hate to answer the telephone. Somehow you always seem to be carrying on these dumb conversations.

"Hello."

"Who is it?"

"It's me."

"Who are you?"

"Who do you want?"

"It depends."

"On what?"

"On if I have the right number."

"What number did you want?"

"What number is this?"

"I asked you first."

One way to avoid getting into a conversation like this is to always answer a "who is it" question by saying, "This is Sybil." (Don't say, "This is

Sybil" if your name isn't Sybil.) Another helpful thing to say is, "Who do you want to speak to?" Or if you are very correct you might say, "To whom do you wish to speak?"

There are all kinds of ways to be polite on the telephone.

How To Answer A Telephone Call

Your mother is soaking in a hot tub and you are just about ready to mix yourself a nice glass of Ovaltine, when the phone rings.

"Hello, I'd like to speak to Morris."

You've been around long enough to know that there is no Morris living in your house. You also know that you don't like to be interrupted in the middle of your Ovaltine, so you would like to say, "Morris doesn't live here," and hang up—hard!

Something tells you that this is being impolite. So you don't do it. You wonder if you should be helpful and tell the man to look in the phone book or try information. That's not necessary. Just say, "Sorry, you have the wrong number."

Now suppose the phone call was not a wrong number:

"Hello, is your mother in?"

"Yes."

"May I please speak to her?"

"No."

"Why not?"

"She's taking a bath with Calgon Bouquet.

Call back when she gets out of the tub."

The way you handled yourself wasn't exactly correct.

First of all, it's nobody's business (except maybe your father's) that your mother is in the bathtub. Secondly, you didn't even find out who called. What if your mother comes out of the tub and asks, "Were there any phone calls?"

You would have to say, "Yes, there were two of them; a wrong number and a lady."

That doesn't tell your mother a whole lot. Maybe the conversation could have gone like this:

"Hello, is your mother in?"

"Yes, but she can't come to the phone right now. May I take a message?"

The caller probably would have told you her name and said, "I'll call back later," or "Ask your mother to call me."

How To Make A Phone Call

You are going to call up Marcia because there's nobody around and you can talk in private. You are also going to impress Marcia's mother with your manners.

"Hello, Mrs. Wertentile. This is Sybil. May I please speak to Marcia?"

Beautiful! How can Mrs. Wertentile resist you? Even if Marcia is in the middle of her homework, and Mrs. Wertentile never lets her talk on the phone during homework time, she might make an

exception. Maybe she'll ask herself, "How can I say no to a polite girl like Sybil?"

But what if Marcia isn't home? You can still be polite.

"Please ask her to call me when she comes home." Or, "Please tell her I'll call back later." Then you say thank you and good-bye, hang up and sit around wondering where Marcia went and why she didn't ask you to go with her.

Showing Telephone Consideration

You're in luck. Marcia is home when you call and she isn't doing her homework. So now you can talk and talk and talk. Sounds like fun; except that maybe your mother or father are waiting to use the phone. Or maybe someone's trying to call your house and can't get through because you're talking so long. Or maybe there is an emergency. Also, extra long phone calls can be very expensive.

So keep your calls short and give someone else a chance to talk. Your mother and father might let you use the phone more often if you do.

If Marcia should ever call you while you have a guest visiting, it would be very impolite to talk and talk and talk while you leave your guest sitting, sitting and sitting. Tell Marcia that you have company and will call her back later.

INTRODUCTIONS

Introductions can turn strangers into friends. It's also nice to know the names of the people you are talking to.

How much do you know about making introductions? Who is introduced to whom? For instance —do you introduce the person you like to the person you don't like? Or the person you don't like to the person you like? The answer is *neither*. Liking and not liking don't have too much to do with introducing.

When we introduce people to each other, we

honor those who are special in some way by saying their names first.

We honor:

1. People who are older.
2. People who hold important titles or positions.
3. Women and girls.

Introducing A Younger Person To An Older Person

It is Monday—the day of your piano lesson. You didn't practice all week, but Miss Muldoon is coming anyway. So is Marcia. She wants to see what a piano lesson looks like. Her mother is thinking of giving her lessons with Miss Muldoon too, because she doesn't charge a whole lot.

You figure it might be polite of you to introduce Marcia to Miss Muldoon. Only what do you say? Do you say, "Miss Muldoon, this is my friend Marcia?" Or do you say, "Marcia, this is Miss Muldoon."

Well, the thing to remember is that *the older person's* name comes first. Even if you like Marcia better, Miss Muldoon's name still comes first. She's older than Marcia, and you should show her some respect. So you say, "Miss Muldoon, this is my friend Marcia." And if you want, you can add, "She's thinking of taking piano lessons too."

Or let's say you have just invited the new girl in your class, Irma Fishbein, to spend the night at

your house. It would be nice of you, a
polite, to introduce Irma to your mothe
won't feel that a stranger is sleeping ov
would introduce Irma to your mother the same
way you introduced Marcia to Miss Muldoon. Your
mother is older, so she comes first. You say, "Mother,
this is Irma Fishbein."

But before Irma is standing in front of your
mother with her toothbrush and pajamas, make
sure you had permission to invite her.

Introducing A Boy To A Girl

This is a good one. Boys have to be introduced
to girls. Ha! It doesn't matter if the boy you are
introducing is a nice boy who lets you alone, or if
he's a creep. The girl comes first.

Suppose your cousin Albert from Minneapolis
is visiting you and you want to make a good impres-
sion. You're going to show him how charming and
polite you have become. Even your mother did a
polite thing. She took Albert's picture out of the
drawer and hung it up on the wall.

Anyway, Albert is visiting and you're trying
to figure out something charming and polite to say,
when who should come over but Irma. This is the
chance you've been waiting for. You say, "Irma,
this is my cousin Albert from Minneapolis."

You figure it's a good idea to add that part
about Minneapolis because it might lead to an interesting discussion about flour mills.

29

To my friend Sybil with best wishes
Mayor Willoughby

Introducing A Less Important Person To A More Important Person

You have written a brilliant essay on citizenship and you are going to receive an award from the mayor. By the end of the ceremony you feel as though you and he are pretty good friends. You even get to shake his hand. So now you are ready to introduce him to everyone you know. Remember, the mayor is the important person, so his name comes first.

"Mayor Willoughby, I'd like you to meet my mother."

"Mayor Willoughby, this is my teacher Mrs. Fingerhut."

"Mayor Willoughby, this is my friend Marcia Wertentile."

"Mayor Willoughby, this is my cousin Albert."

Your mother and father are important people too. But when you introduce them to other adults, the polite thing to do is say the other person's name first.

"Mrs. Fingerhut, this is my mother."

"Mr. Wertentile, this is my father."

Be sure to say your mother's or father's last name if it's different from yours.

Making the proper introductions might seem to be a bit confusing at times. That's because they are. But with a little practice you'll get so good, you'll hardly ever mess things up.

How To Act When You Are Being Introduced

Some people don't know how to act when they are being introduced. Take Irma and Albert for instance. They never did get around to talking about flour mills. In fact, they didn't even say hello. While you were doing a superb job of introducing, Albert cracked his knuckles and looked up at the ceiling, and Irma sat on the couch, twiddling her fat thumbs.

Probably nobody ever told Irma and Albert what to do when someone introduces them.

Let's say you are sprawled out on the couch

reading a great book on the life cycle of a fruit fly, when your mother gets a visitor—a lady she's known since fifth grade.

"Sybil, come here, dear. I'd like to introduce you to a lady I've known since fifth grade."

What do you do?

1. Act like you didn't hear and go right on reading.
2. Wave from the couch and go right on reading.
3. Say, "Hi," and go right on reading.
4. Stand up and get ready to be introduced.

If you stood up, you did the polite thing. You should always stand up when you're being introduced. And even when you're not being introduced, it's nice to stand up whenever an adult enters the room.

Now that you're standing and being polite, what do you do when your mother says, "Virginia, this is my daughter, Sybil. Sybil, this is Mrs. Higgenbottom."

Do you—

1. Scratch your head?
2. Clear your throat?
3. Say, "Can I go back to the couch now?"
4. Smile and say, "Hello, Mrs. Higgenbottom."

If you said, "Hello, Mrs. Higgenbottom," you made your mother very happy. She got a chance to show Mrs. Higgenbottom what a good job she did in bringing you up.

And one more thing. Did you remember to look directly at Mrs. Higgenbottom? Smiling and saying hello don't mean too much if you're looking down at the floor or across the room, wishing you were back on the couch with your fruit flies.

CONVERSATIONS

You Can Help People Start Conversations

When you introduced Marcia to Miss Muldoon, did you add, "She's thinking of taking piano lessons too." If so, you did a very smart thing. Marcia and Miss Muldoon would have something to talk about.

You also did a smart thing by telling Irma that Albert comes from Minneapolis. They could have had that great discussion about flour mills. It's not your fault that they didn't get the hint. Most people like to begin their own conversations—to find out for themselves what somebody else thinks or does. But other people have trouble getting a conversation started. If you think this might be the case, you can help them by adding a little something to your introductions.

For instance, you can—

1. Tell Mayor Willoughby that your cousin Albert would like to become mayor of Minneapolis.

2. Tell Mayor Willoughby that Marcia is wondering if the circus is coming to town this year.
3. Tell Mayor Willoughby that your mother is very concerned about air pollution.
4. Tell Mrs. Fingerhut that your mother thinks teaching is a nice career for a girl.

How To Start Your Own Conversations

What do you do if there's nobody around to introduce you to another person? What if nobody helps you get a conversation started? How do you start your own?

Remember the day you first met Irma? It was recess time and you and a bunch of girls were standing around talking, when you noticed Irma sitting all alone on a bench. You don't like to see people sitting by themselves, so you went over to talk to her.

"Hi," you said. "I'm Sybil Macintosh."

"I'm Irma Fishbein," she answered.

Then you ask her a few questions—like where did she come from, and how did she like the school so far, and what did she think of Mrs. Fingerhut.

You introduced her to the rest of the girls so she could get to know everyone. And you and Irma

34

have been good friends ever since.

You can also start a conversation by—

1. Giving an honest compliment.
   "You look nice with your hair parted in the middle."
2. Asking about a hobby.
   "How long have you been collecting butterflies?"

You Should Not Ask Questions That Are None Of Your Business

Remember the time when you and Marcia and Irma had a discussion about how people sleep? You said you slept on your side, and Marcia said she slept on her back, and Irma said she slept on her stomach.

The three of you began to wonder which was the most common way to sleep. So you went from door to door to find out. But every time you asked somebody, "Do you sleep on your side, on your back or on your stomach?" you had the door slammed in your faces.

You thought people were being impolite. But the reason this happened is because you asked a question that was none of your business.

Other questions that are none of your business are:

1. "How much did your dress cost?"
2. "Does your mother wear false teeth?"

3. "Did your father quit his job or was he fired?"

Know When To Interrupt A Conversation

Some people can go on talking forever. At times you might find it necessary to interrupt a person so that you can help carry on a more lively and interesting conversation. But try not to get into the habit of constantly interrupting others, never giving them a chance to finish talking. By doing this, you are telling people that you think you're the only one who has something important to say.

Don't Brag

Somebody made the mistake of asking you how your piano lessons are coming along. You told everyone what a great genius you are—a regular Mozart —and you don't even practice. You're so great, you couldn't stop talking about yourself.

If you're really as good as you say you are, there's no need to brag. People will find out for themselves.

Don't Exaggerate

Sometimes you get the urge to liven up a conversation by making up stories:

You were witness to a bank robbery and you used your walkie-talkie to make contact with the police and you received a reward for five hundred dollars.

36

...AND THEN MAYOR WILLOUGHBY SAID TO ME, HE SAID, "SYBIL, YOU HAVE ONE OF THE FINEST ANALYTICAL MINDS I'VE EVER SEEN!" HE SAID, "YOU SHOULD GO INTO POL- ITICS, YOU'D PROBABLY BECOME THE FIRST WOMAN PRESIDENT!" AND THEN HE SAID "SYBIL MY DEAR," HE SAID, "YOU HAVE REALLY BEAUTI- FUL EYES! THEY REMIND ME OF FOREST POOLS AT SUNSET!" MAYOR WILLOUGH- BY REALLY WAS IMPRESSED BY WHAT I WAS WEARING, TOO. HE SAID "SY- BIL" HE SAID, "THAT COLOR BRINGS OUT THE LOVELY COLOR OF YOUR HAIR." THEN HE SAID...

Or

You were walking along a dark alley when you fell into an open manhole where you were trapped for eighteen hours without food or water until you were rescued by a troop of boy scouts who were going on a hike.

Or

The President of the United States personally invited you and your parents to the Inaugural Ball, but you couldn't go because your father had to work late and you had to study for a spelling test.

Or

You were in the amusement park riding on a ferris wheel and it kept going round and round for ten hours without stopping and you didn't even get dizzy.

If you keep exaggerating like this, how will people be able to believe the things that really do happen to you?

Be A Good Listener

One of the reasons you and Marcia get along so well is that you like talking to each other. You like listening to each other too.

Marcia always seems to be interested in what you have to say. She looks straight at you and makes comments at just the right times.

Irma is a pretty good listener, but not as good as Marcia. Sometimes Irma seems to be thinking

38

about something else while you're talking. And sometimes she looks across the room to see who else is around. So most of the time you talk to Marcia instead of Irma.

SAYING EXCUSE ME

Sometimes it is necessary to say *excuse me*. You should say *excuse me* when—

1. You are trying to find a seat in a movie theater and have to pass in front of people.
2. You have to cut in front of a person.
3. You are moving through a crowd.
4. You yawn in someone's face.
5. You have to interrupt your mother while she's talking to a friend.

By saying *excuse me*, you show a person that you know you have disturbed him in some way and that it matters to you.

APOLOGIZING

For Something You Said

You and Marcia were on your way back from another shopping trip at Woolworth's when you stopped to take a pebble out of your shoe.

Marcia watched you for a while and then she said, "Gee, Sybil, you sure have dirty shoes."

You didn't like what she said about your shoes,

so you said, "Gee, Marcia, you sure have big feet."

Marcia started to cry and ran home, while you were left wondering if you should have said that.

What Marcia said about your shoes wasn't very nice. But what you said about Marcia's feet was much worse. Marcia really does have big feet. And she knows it. You can always clean your shoes, but there's nothing much she can do about her feet; except maybe to get her bones shortened, and that involves a major operation.

You could just picture Marcia crying somewhere—all because of something you said. So you rushed home, picked up the phone and dialed the number. Then you said, "Hi, Marcia. I'm sorry."

For Something You Did

You and Albert got into a fight and it was all your fault.

You yelled at Albert for cracking his knuckles and looking up at the ceiling when he should have been saying hello to Irma and talking about flour mills.

Then you socked him in the arm and the fight started. Albert threw you on the ground and sat on you until you agreed to apologize for yelling and socking.

You realized you were wrong, and besides that, your ribs were hurting. So you looked at Albert and said, "I'm sorry."

For Something You Didn't Do

You promised to take Bruce to the candy store right after school, but you forgot. You went home with Marcia instead.

Later on, you remembered Bruce and the candy store and your broken promise. So you went over to Bruce's house and said, "I'm sorry I forgot to take you today, Bruce. But we'll go tomorrow—for sure."

You should also say *I'm sorry* when—

1. You are looking for your seat in a movie theater and step on someone's toes.
2. You are running wildly to your room because you're tardy, and bump into Mrs. Fingerhut.
3. You are tapping, "Mary Had A Little Lamb," on your mother's favorite glasses, and you break one because you tapped too hard.
4. You accidently trip someone on the school bus.

An apology can never undo what's been done, but it's better than nothing. It lets the other person know you care.

CHAPTER TWO

TABLE MANNERS

Albert has gone back to Minneapolis. Before he left, he invited you to his house for spring vacation.

Your mother said you can go—on one condition—you have to improve your table manners. She's afraid you'll embarass her. You can't understand why your mother is so worried about you. You've seen Albert eat and he doesn't have any table manners either. But you're very anxious to go to Minneapolis, so you've agreed to give the manners a try.

Cleaning Up For Meals

You've just finished helping Bruce dig to China. Bruce is still digging, but it's dinner time and you're starved. You rush straight from the dirt pile to the dining room table, plop into your chair and yell, "What's for dinner?"

It's lucky for you that you can't see yourself—you would have spoiled your appetite. But your mother sees you, and she chases you into the bathroom to wash up.

It's not only unattractive to be dirty at mealtime, but it's also very bad for your health. Dirt contains germs. You can't see them, but they are there—all ready to invade your body. And we won't even talk about worms.

If you keep forgetting to wash your hands and face before eating, just think about germs and worms. They're easy words to remember because they rhyme.

Setting The Table

A good way to get to the food in a hurry is to help your mother set the table.

Whether you eat on fancy china (this *china* means dishes, not the country) or on plastic, you set the table the same way. You use whatever forks, spoons and knives that each person will need for the meal. And you place them in a way that will be attractive and convenient to use.

Place the fork to the left of the plate. Place the folded napkin to the left of the fork. Place the knife to the right of the plate, with its cutting side toward the plate. Place the spoon to the right of the knife. The drinking glass should be just above the knife and spoon.

Dear Mom
Well Hi! I set
the table because
I knew you'd be
late, coming home
from your Karate lesson!
I broke your favorite
wine glass, by the way.
Love
Sybil

The Napkin

The napkin should be kept on your lap in case of an emergency (remember the noodle soup?).

Let's suppose you have just dipped your hand in the salad dressing. What should you do?

1. Wipe the dressing on the tablecloth.
2. Lick it off.
3. Wipe it on your dress.
4. Wipe it on your napkin.

Number four is correct. You should also use the napkin to wipe your greasy mouth before you take a drink. Otherwise you'll get your glass all messy. You should wipe your mouth after taking a drink too.

Forks, Spoons, Fingers and Knives

There are times when you're not sure if you should eat with a fork, a spoon, or with your fingers. You can either look around to see what everybody else is doing, or you can just use common sense.

Most foods are eaten with a fork. Forks are also used for cutting soft foods.

But picture yourself eating soup with a fork —or with your fingers.

Soup and other moist foods should be eaten with a spoon. Here is a list of some of the foods that should be eaten with a spoon:

    cereal
    chocolate pudding (it doesn't *have* to be
        chocolate)
    fruit cocktail
    grapefruit halves
    ice cream

Sometimes you get lucky and can use your fingers. Just about any kind of food that does not mess up your hands and face can be eaten with your fingers. Some finger foods are:

    potato chips
    bread
    crackers
    cookies
    dry cake (for strawberry shortcake, use a
    fork)
    olives
    carrot and celery sticks

corn on the cob

sandwiches

One of the reasons you know that Albert has no table manners is because he puts knives in his mouth. Albert likes to line up little green peas along his knife to see how many he can get into his mouth before they roll off.

It's not only impolite to put a knife in your mouth, it's also very dangerous. Knives are used only for cutting (meat) and spreading (butter, jelly and cheese).

GOING TO SOMEONE'S HOUSE FOR DINNER

Marcia's mother has invited you to dinner for Thursday evening. Your father is giving you some last minute instructions.

"Don't forget to sit up straight, Sybil."

Your father knows all about your habit of tilting the chair backwards to see how far you can lean before you fall. He also knows how you like to sit all hunched over, so that you can stick your face in the dish while you're eating.

When sitting at a table, your own or someone else's, you should sit up straight. Your feet should be flat on the floor, not wrapped around the legs of the chair. You should not try to play footsies with Marcia. You might find out that you were playing footsies with Marcia's father instead.

"Don't tap 'Mary Had A Little Lamb' on the glasses."

You ask your father if it's okay to tap "Twinkle, Twinkle Little Star." But he says you shouldn't do any tapping at all. You might break Mrs. Wertentile's glasses. And besides, tapping disturbs people.

Humming at the table and playing with the silverware are also disturbing. You should sit quietly with your hands in your lap until dinner is served.

DINNER IS SERVED

You arrived at Marcia's house on time, and you are at the table sitting up straight. So far you have been very polite. But a problem has just come up. Mrs. Wertentile didn't set the table the way you usually do. She put out two forks and two spoons. You're very confused. What do you use, and when do you use it?

The fork farthest from the plate is the first fork to be used. The spoon farthest from the plate is the first spoon to be used; that's assuming Mrs. Wertentile knows how to set a table correctly. Better yet, wait until others begin and watch what they do.

What To Do If You Don't Like A Certain Food

Mrs. Wertentile offers you some cole slaw. You don't especially like cole slaw. What do you do?

1. Say, "I don't like cole slaw."
2. Say, "Cabbage gives me gas."

3. Say, "No thank you."

4. Take a small amount.

If you chose number three or number four, you would be safe. It's all right to refuse a food by saying, "No thank you." It's also polite to take a small amount even if you aren't sure you'll eat it.

If Mrs. Wertentile gives you your plate with the food already on it, don't make any comments. Eat what you like and leave what you don't like.

When To Start Eating

Your plate is filled and you are starved. At home you would plunge right in. But what do you do at Marcia's house?

To be polite, you should wait until Marcia or Marcia's mother or father are ready to eat—unless Mrs. Wertentile gives you a go-ahead signal.

Passing The Food

The bread basket is right in front of you, and Marcia wants a roll. "Pass me a roll, Sybil, please." What do you do?

1. Pick out a roll and throw it across the table.

2. Pick out a roll and hand it to Marcia.

3. Pass the whole basket to Marcia.

If you picked number three you were right. Never pass individual pieces of food. Always pass the whole serving dish.

49

When you want something that isn't near you, never reach across the table. You can say—

"Please pass the salt, Marcia."

"May I please have some potatoes, Mrs. Wertentile?"

Don't use your own fork when you help yourself to the potatoes. Use the serving fork if it's there; otherwise ask Marcia's mother for one.

Some "Don'ts" For Your Mouth

1. Don't put too much food in your mouth.
2. Don't chew with your mouth open.
3. Don't talk with your mouth full.
4. Don't drink with your mouth full.
5. Don't blow on your food to cool it.
6. Don't make loud eating noises.

50

Embarassing Situations

Mrs. Wertentile passes you the olives. You love olives—green ones and black ones. Only what do you do with the olive pit once you've eaten the olive?

1. Keep it in your mouth.
2. Swallow it.
3. Hide it in your napkin.
4. Take it out of your mouth and put it on your plate.

You have to read the next question before you get the answer to this one.

What do you do if you find yourself eating a fishbone?

1. Yell, "Help! A fishbone!"
2. Swallow it and hope you don't choke.
3. Spit it into your napkin.
4. Take it out of your mouth and put it on your plate.

These two questions have the same answer—number four. You treat olive pits and fishbones the same way. Remove a pit or bone with your thumb and forefinger (the finger you point with), and place it on your plate.

If you are eating canned or cooked fruit (cherries, for example) with a spoon, use the spoon to remove the pits.

You find a hair in your mashed potatoes. What do you do?

1. Say, "Look what I found."
2. Look around to see whose head it matches.
3. Say, "Ick, hair in my potatoes."
4. Don't say anything and eat the rest of the food.

Number four is the right answer. You wouldn't want to embarass Mrs. Wertentile, so don't say anything about the hair. Besides, the hair might be yours.

What do you do if you put food in your mouth that is too hot?

1. Swallow fast.
2. Spit it out.
3. Yell, "Help! I'm on fire!"
4. Take a quick swallow of water (or whatever else there is to drink).

Number four is just about the only thing you can do.

Suppose a piece of food is stuck in your teeth. What do you do?

1. Try to get it out with your tongue.
2. Try to get it out with your fingers.
3. Ask Mrs. Wertentile for a toothpick.
4. Wait until later when you are alone.

Number four is right. It is always impolite to try to remove food from your teeth in front of other people.

Accidents Will Happen

Accidents happen all the time. Even Mrs. Wertentile had an accident. She dropped one of her best forks down the garbage disposal. So if a minor accident occurs during mealtime, don't get upset.

Some common mealtime accidents are:

1. Spilling a glass of water.
    Say, "I'm sorry," and Mrs. Wertentile will clean it up.
2. Dropping a piece of roast beef in Mr. Wertentile's lap.
    Say, "I'm sorry," and Mr. and Mrs. Wertentile will clean it up.
3. Dropping your napkin.
    Pick it up.
4. Dropping your fork under the table.
    Ask for another one (you can pick it up after the meal).
5. Dropping a piece of food on the table.
    Pick it up and put it on the side of your plate.
6. Dropping a piece of food on the floor.
    Leave it there (maybe Mrs. Wertentile will think Marcia did it).

Eating Foods That Are Hard To Handle

What if Mrs. Wertentile serves something that's hard to handle? For example:

1. Corn on the cob
   Butter a few rows at a time so it won't drip all over you.
2. Watermelon
   Remove the pits with a fork. You can either eat the watermelon with a fork or hold it in your hands.
3. Spaghetti
   If you have a hard time winding it around your fork like a professional, cut it into smaller pieces with the fork.
4. Soup
   Remember the noodle soup in your lap? This time, dip the spoon *away* from you. Bring the spoon up to your mouth. Don't duck your head into the soup. Don't blow on it or slurp.

Second Helpings

Mrs. Wertentile says, "Have some more mashed potatoes, Sybil."

You would just love a second helping, so you take some.

Mrs. Wertentile says, "Have some more carrots, Sybil."

You don't want any more carrots, so you say, "No thank you."

Mrs. Wertentile gives you the carrots anyway. Guess what? Mrs. Wertentile has just wasted food. You don't have to eat them.

Avoiding Unpleasant Remarks

You like your roast beef well-done. Marcia likes hers rare. You can't understand how she can eat such rare meat. She also likes catsup on her potatoes. Don't say "Ick! How can you eat meat with all that blood on it?" or, "Catsup on potatoes?"

Just keep quiet. You eat what you like, and let Marcia eat what she likes.

Mealtime Conversations

Pleasant conversations can make dining more enjoyable. But mealtime is not the time to:

1. Talk about the dead bird you saw lying in the street.
2. Tell how you threw up on the school bus.
3. Show the infected sore on your elbow.
4. Explain the digestive process, starting with the teeth and going all the way down to the large intestine.

Excusing Yourself During An Emergency

Ordinarily, you should stay at the table until the meal has ended and you are excused. But what if you simply *have* to go to the bathroom. Or what if you have a piece of food stuck in your teeth and it's driving you crazy?

If an emergency occurs, simply say, "Excuse me," and leave the table. Don't explain where you're going and why.

The Meal Has Ended

You are finished eating. What do you do with your napkin?

> **1.** Put it on your plate to cover up the food you left.
> **2.** Fold it carefully so Mrs. Wertentile will think you are a neat eater and didn't have to use it.
> **3.** Ask Mrs. Wertentile where she keeps the dirty laundry.
> **4.** Put it on the table next to your plate.

Number four is the right answer. And make sure your napkin isn't all crumpled.

What do you do with your knife and fork?

> **1.** Put them on the table because the tablecloth is probably dirty anyway.
> **2.** Stick them into a piece of meat you've been saving for that purpose.
> **3.** Balance them on the edge of your plate.
> **4.** Lay them across your plate.

The last answer was the right one. That way they won't fall off the plate when Mrs. Wertentile is cleaning up.

When Do You Leave The Table?

You may leave the table when you are excused, or when Marcia or her parents leave.

If you are totally confused by all these rules,

just remember—whenever you're dining at some-one's home, and you're not sure what to do about something, watch to see what the host and hostess do, and just hope they know what they're doing.

Before you go home, don't forget to say good-bye to Marcia's mother and father, and thank them for inviting you.

EATING AT A RESTAURANT

You're going to a restaurant and you're thrilled. So are your parents. For a change they won't have to cook and wash dishes.

The restaurant is a fancy one. You are shown to your table and given a menu. You have a hard time reading the menu because it's written mostly in French. So your mother and father help you and make suggestions.

After you ask your father to order you a ham-burger, you sit around and watch people eat. It's interesting to see what goes on at the other tables. You're right in the middle of watching two ladies chewing, when your father says, "Sybil, stop staring. Don't you know it's impolite to watch people eat?"

Your father is right. At a restaurant you have to resist the temptation to be nosy. You have to try not to pay too much attention to what's going on at the other tables.

Eating at a restaurant is a lot like eating at someone's house. But in some ways it's different.

Here are some questions that might come up

when you're in the restaurant.

> **Q.** What if you find a hair in your food?
> Or a fly? Or what if the food tastes
> like it's been poisoned?
>
> **A.** If you find anything wrong with your
> food, don't eat it. You don't have to
> worry about hurting the restaurant's
> feelings. Just tell your mother and
> father, and they will ask the waiter to
> replace the food.
>
> **Q.** What if your fork is dirty?
>
> **A.** Don't wipe it off. Tell your mother
> and father, and they will have the
> waiter get you a new one.
>
> **Q.** What if you drop a fork (or spoon, or
> knife) on the floor?
>
> **A.** Leave it there. You don't need to pick
> it up. Your parents will ask for an-
> other one.

Going To A Restaurant Without Your Mother And Father

You and Marcia and Irma like to go out together—mostly for hot fudge sundaes. The place
you go isn't a restaurant exactly; it's more like an
ice cream shop. But it's sort of like a restaurant
because you sit at tables and there's a waitress to
serve you.

If you have a lot of books or packages, don't

pile them up on the table. Keep them under the table or right next to your chair (make sure the waitress can't trip over them).

Order your sundae politely. "I'll have a hot fudge sundae, please." Or if you order for the three of you, "We'll have three hot fudge sundaes, please."

What do you do if you drop your spoon while you're eating your sundae?

1. Pick it up and wipe it off.
2. Leave it there and eat the whipped cream with your fingers.
3. Wait until Marcia finishes her sundae and use her spoon.
4. Politely ask the waitress for another spoon.

Number four is the correct answer, of course.

In the middle of her hot fudge sundae, Marcia starts to comb her hair. You remind her that it's very impolite to comb her hair at the table, but she says it's an emergency. The emergency, as you see it, is a sixth-grade boy named Harvey, who has just walked into the ice cream shop.

You tell Marcia, "Harvey or no Harvey, you shouldn't comb your hair at the table." So Marcia hurries to the rest room, and by the time she gets out, Harvey is sitting with a girl from the sixth grade.

The three of you pick up your books from under the table, pay the check and go home.

CHAPTER THREE

PARTIES

Giving A Party

Congratulations! It's your birthday and you're having a party. Your mother has given you permission to invite all thirteen girls in your class for cake and ice cream on a Sunday afternoon. You tell her thirteen is an unlucky number, so you'll just ask twelve. You figure you'll leave Phyllis out because you don't like her too much anyway.

Your mother says, "No Phyllis, no party."

Some party. It hasn't even begun yet, and your mother is already telling you who you can invite and who you can't. She doesn't even know Phyllis, so why do you have to invite her?

Your mother has a good reason. Think of how you would feel if you were the only girl in your class who wasn't invited to a party. It's all right to ask some girls and not ask others. But if you ask all, then ask ALL. Once Phyllis is in your house, you might even decide you like her.

The Invitations

You can either invite your guests by telephone, or send them written invitations. Sometimes written invitations are better because the girls will have something to pin up on their bulletin boards—and it'll be easier for them to remember the exact time and date of your party.

Don't send the invitations out two months ahead of time. Everyone will forget all about you by then. A week or two before the party is enough time to do your inviting.

Whether you make up your own invitations, or buy printed cards with blank spaces to be filled in, don't forget to include:

1. your name
2. your address
3. your telephone number
4. the date
5. the time

And be sure to let everyone know it's a birthday party so no one will forget to bring a present.

Plan Your Party

If you don't want your guests to just sit around

doing nothing, the way Irma and Albert did, be sure to plan your party beforehand. Decide what games you'll play, when the refreshments will be served and when you'll open the presents.

Answering The Door

The doorbell rings. You answer it, and who should be standing there but your friend, Dorothy, from down the block. You decided to invite Dorothy because she's nice, and because you still didn't like the idea of sending out thirteen invitations.

Your first impulse is to grab the present and leave Dorothy standing alone in the doorway. Control yourself. Of course you're anxious to see what she brought you, but the time to open the package will come soon enough. Besides, a little suspense will make the present even more exciting.

First say hello and invite Dorothy into the house. Then you can take the present and say thank you, while you show her where to put her coat (if she's wearing a coat).

Dorothy doesn't know all the girls in your class because she's a grade ahead of you. So you should introduce her to anybody she's unfamiliar with.

Taking Care Of Your Guests

There's more to giving a party than sending out invitations, serving refreshments, and opening presents.

The most important job you have as hostess is

GOSH, SYBIL! DO YOU HAVE TO SPIT?

to see that everyone has a good time; that no one is all alone and left out of the fun.

Dorothy doesn't know too many girls, so you might have to pay a little more attention to her if she seems to need it.

Some girls are more shy than others, and it's up to you to see that they have someone to talk to or something to do.

Seating Arrangements

If all of the girls will be sitting down at one large table, it's a good idea to write their names on place cards. That way you can seat the girls next to people they're friendly with. Dorothy knows Marcia and Irma, so maybe she can sit with them instead

of sitting next to girls she doesn't know.

If you serve buffet style (the food and plates are on a table and the girls serve themselves), arrange the chairs into cozy groups so that no one will be sitting all alone.

Don't force your birthday cake on anyone, but see to it that whoever wants a piece gets it.

If there is enough cake left after everyone has had a first helping, offer seconds—or thirds.

Serving The Refreshments

The candles were lit, your friends sang, "Happy birthday, dear Sybil," and now you're ready to eat.

There are four flowers on your cake and all the girls are crying, "Ooh, Sybil, can I have one?"

Even though you're not the greatest in math, you know very well that fifteen girls (fifteen includes you) can't each have a flower if there are only four flowers. So what do you do?

1. Eat one flower and give the other three to Marcia, Irma and Dorothy because you like them best.
2. Eat all four by yourself because you can't play favorites.
3. Give each girl part of a flower.

If you gave each girl part of a flower, good for you. You made everyone happy. A petal is better than no flower at all.

Phyllis just dropped her cake on the carpet. What do you do?

1. Yell at her for being so clumsy.
2. Let her clean up the mess by herself.
3. Leave it there for your mother.
4. Help her clean it up and give her a new piece.

Phyllis probably feels bad enough about the accident. Don't make her feel worse. Smile and say, "That's all right, Phyllis. It can be cleaned up." Then do answer number four.

Playing Games

You've spent a whole week planning original

games for your party. You've bought some terrific prizes to give away to the winners—and you expect to do a lot of winning.

You can play all the games you want to. But you're the hostess, and the games are for the entertainment of your guests. So if you win, don't keep the prize. And don't give it to Marcia or Irma just because they're your best friends. Give it to the runner-up—even if it's Phyllis. And if you lose, don't cry.

Opening Presents

This is the moment you've been waiting for. You're all ready to open your presents, and while you're trying to decide where to begin, all the girls are yelling, "Open mine first!" What do you do?

1. Open Marcia's present first, Irma's present second, Dorothy's present third, and Phyllis's present last.
2. Open the prettiest packages first.
3. Open the biggest packages first.
4. Just pick at random.

You were right if you chose number four. It's important to treat all presents equally, so don't make a big thing out of which one to open first. If you'd like, you can begin by opening the ones closest to you.

Every time you open a gift, tell who it's from and show it to the girls. Then be sure to say thank

67

you to the giver. While you're opening all your
presents, watch out for such comments as:

> **1.** "Now THIS I like."
>   (you don't like the others)
> **2.** "This is the best present ever."
>   (all the other presents aren't as good)

You have just opened your fourth comb and
brush set—this one is from Phyllis. What do you
say?

> **1.** "Oh, no. Not another one."

2. "How many combs and brushes do I need?"
3. "I only have one head."
4. "Thank you, Phyllis."

Number four of course. Never hurt a person's feelings by expressing disappointment in a gift. After all, the giving of the gift, and the thought that goes with it is more important than the gift itself.

Saying Good-bye

The party is almost over. You've eaten, played some games, and opened your presents. All that's left is the dancing. You're right in the middle of inventing a new dance step, when Dorothy tells you she has to go home.

You know you should walk her to the door the way you walked Marcia to the door when she was having milk and cookies at your house. But you know you're also supposed to entertain your guests. So what do you do?

When a person is ready to leave your party, it's all right to desert your other guests while you say good-bye. So you help Dorothy get her coat (if she wore a coat) and walk her to the door. You say, "I'm glad you came to my party, Dorothy. And thanks for the present."

With Phyllis it's a different story. You're not at all glad she came to your party, but you can still be polite. "Good-bye, Phyllis. It was nice of you to come. Thank you for the gift."

Going To A Party

You get a telephone call from Irma.

"Hi, Sybil. I'm having a slumber party Saturday night. Can you come? It'll be from seven o'clock until ten o'clock Sunday morning."

"Who else is gonna be there?"

"Marcia, my cousin Bibbi, and Dorothy." (Dorothy and Irma have become pretty good friends ever since they sat next to each other at your birthday party.)

"Okay, in that case I'll come."

You just made two mistakes:

1. Before you even accepted the invitation, you were already checking out the guest list. Wait until you've definitely accepted before you ask, "Who else is gonna be there?"
2. You told Irma you can come to her party. How do you know you can? Did you ask your parents? Before accepting an invitation, you should get permission from your mother or father—depending upon who's in charge of permission for parties.

Answering The Invitation

All invitations should be answered promptly and definitely. So ask your mother if you can go to Irma's slumber party. If she says yes, you call Irma

70

back and say, "I can come to your party, Irma."

If she says you can't go because you're going away for the weekend, you call back and say, "I'm sorry, Irma, but I won't be able to come to the party. We're going away for the weekend."

Never keep a person waiting for an answer to an invitation. And never ignore an invitation completely. Those are good ways to get yourself uninvited to parties.

Going To The Party

Lucky for you the answer was yes. You can go to Irma's party.

You're only going for one night, so you don't have to pack a trunk. But don't come unprepared either, expecting to borrow Irma's pajamas. Pack an overnight case with—

1. pajamas or nightgown
2. robe and slippers
3. comb and brush
4. toothbrush and toothpaste

If you put on some clean clothes right before you go to Irma's house, you can wear the same things the next morning.

At The Party

Before you rush into Irma's house to get into your pajamas, say hello first. If it's Irma's birthday (it's not), give her the present and say, "Happy birthday, Irma." And don't forget to say hello to Irma's mother and father.

Irma will let everyone know when to change into pajamas. Don't make any cracks about Dorothy's pajamas or Marcia's nightie.

And make sure your clothes aren't scattered all over Irma's house.

Refreshments

You need your table manners even at a slumber party, and even when you're not eating at a table. So when Irma's mother serves the tuna salad sandwiches, potato chips, and milk, eat neatly. If you

drop any food on the floor, do your best to clean it up.

Being A Good Sport

Irma has all sorts of good things planned for her slumber party, but her cousin Bibbi has all sorts of complaints to go with them:

1. "Are we just gonna sit here and talk all night?"
2. "Don't you have any *good* records?"
3. "I don't wanna play any more baby games."
4. "What a dumb prize!"

After spending an evening with Bibbi and her complaints, you have come to an important conclusion: a bad sport can spoil a good party.

Sleeping Arrangements

The plans are for all of you to sleep in the living room. Irma and Bibbi are cousins, so they'll sleep on the sofa that turns into a bed. Marcia was smart and brought her alligator sleeping bag. You and Dorothy have to sleep on the floor.

At first it seems like fun to sleep on the floor. But the longer you lie there, the more uncomfortable it gets. If you want to continue being a good guest though, you won't complain.

While you are trying hard not to complain, Bibbi and Marcia are having an argument. Bibbi wants a night light, and Marcia, who is lying in her sleeping bag with her head sticking out of the alligator's mouth, says she can't sleep with a light on. Irma finally gives Bibbi a flashlight to shine under the covers.

Before you get to sleep there's a lot of giggling to do. But you have to be careful not to giggle all night—Mr. and Mrs. Fishbein need their sleep.

Going Home

You should be ready to go home at ten o'clock, after breakfast. That's when the party's over. Don't hang around for lunch and dinner—unless Mrs.

74

Fishbein asks you to, and you get your mother's permission.

As it turns out, Mrs. Fishbein doesn't ask you and you're glad. You'd like to go home and get some sleep. So you say good-bye to Irma and her mother and father, and thank them. And don't forget to add, "I had a wonderful time."

CHAPTER FOUR

VISITING

You're off to Minneapolis. It's spring vacation, and for one whole week you can forget about school, Mrs. Fingerhut, and Miss Muldoon.

All the arrangements have been made. Your mother and father will put you on the train, and Aunt Agnes (that's Albert's mother) and Uncle Harry (that's Albert's father) will meet you when the train pulls into Minneapolis.

Packing Your Suitcase

For the week in Minneapolis, you will need all the things you took to Irma's house and some changes of clothing and underwear (you can't borrow Albert's). You might want to take a pen along in case you decide to send some postcards to Marcia and Irma and your mother and father.

Bringing A Present

It's always nice to bring a small gift to your host (Albert) and to your host's mother (Aunt Agnes). Or if you prefer, you can send the gifts after you return home.

Some examples of gifts that can be given are:

1. Books—for somebody who likes to read.
2. Stationery—for somebody who likes to write.
3. Candy—for somebody who likes to eat.

Aunt Agnes likes to read and she likes to cook. So you're bringing her a cookbook. Albert likes to fly kites, and he's interested in bats. So you're bringing him a genuine plastic kite shaped like a bat.

Taking Care Of Your Belongings

Aunt Agnes will probably show you where to put your clothes and other belongings. Then make sure everything is kept in the closet and drawers provided for you.

Try not to do any borrowing unless it's absolutely necessary—like a thermometer if you think you have a fever, or an aspirin if you have a headache.

Being Helpful

It would be nice of you to help Aunt Agnes as much as possible. You can help her by making your bed and keeping your room neat. You can also help by setting the table and doing the dishes. But don't insist on helping Aunt Agnes if she doesn't want you to.

Being Considerate

If you want to be a considerate guest—

1. Don't live in the bathroom—other people have to use the bathroom too. So do what you have to do, and get out.
2. Don't mess up the bathroom by leaving your soggy towels and washcloths lying around all over the place. Hang up your soggy towels and washcloths neatly. Wash out the tub after you take a bath, and don't leave your toothpaste all over the sink.
3. Don't insist on watching all your favorite TV programs.
4. Don't use the telephone without permission. If you want to call home, call "collect." (That means your father pays for the call—not Uncle Harry.)
5. Stay out of the refrigerator unless Aunt Agnes tells you to help yourself whenever you get hungry.
6. Don't turn the heat up or down to suit you. If Aunt Agnes likes to keep a cool house, that's her business. If you feel

like you might freeze to death, wear a sweater. If the house is too warm for you, wear light clothing, drink a lot of water, and suffer in silence.

7. Don't complain about the meals. So far you've been lucky. Aunt Agnes makes the best sunny-side up eggs you've ever tasted. But even if she didn't, the polite thing to do would be to eat them and suffer in silence.

Fitting In With The Routine

No two families do things the exact same way. So while you're staying with Albert, Aunt Agnes and Uncle Harry, you'll have to do what they do.

Let's suppose you like to sleep late during your vacation—say until noon—and Aunt Agnes serves breakfast at eight. If you expect to get any breakfast, you should be up and ready to eat by eight. Don't expect Aunt Agnes to prepare a special breakfast for you at lunchtime.

Or let's suppose you are an early riser. You like to watch the sun come up. Don't expect Aunt Agnes, Uncle Harry and Albert to get up early just to watch the sun with you. And if you're hungry, all you can do is wait until they wake up (unless Aunt Agnes tells you to help yourself to the Corn Flakes). Don't help wake them either—by playing piano, singing or turning on the TV.

Respecting Privacy

It's impolite to poke around in closets and drawers to see if you can find some deep, dark secrets about Aunt Agnes and Uncle Harry. It's also impolite to read any letters you see lying around and to listen in on Albert's conversations.

You should respect your parents' privacy too. So don't tell Aunt Agnes and Uncle Harry *everything* that goes on at home—like the time your mother and father had an argument and didn't talk to each other for two days, or how your mother was hoping you wouldn't relearn bad table manners from Albert. Certain things should be kept to yourself.

Accidents

You have just overwound Aunt Agnes's alarm clock because you wanted to be sure to wake up in time for breakfast. What do you do?

1. Act like you don't know what happened.
2. Hide the clock under the bed.
3. Say, "Albert did it."
4. Tell Aunt Agnes what happened and say, "I'm sorry."

Number four might not be an easy thing to do, but it's the only thing to do. Aunt Agnes will find out sooner or later anyway.

Showing Appreciation

Don't be a grouch. Always try to show appreciation for everything that's done for you. For example—

1. When Albert takes you kite flying.
2. When Aunt Agnes takes you shopping.
3. When Uncle Harry takes a day off from work to show you some of the ten thousand lakes in Minnesota.

Saying Good-bye

The week has flown by, and all in all it's been fun. You only had one fight with Albert—the time you got his kite stuck up in a tree.

Your suitcase is packed, and you've seen to it

that none of your things is left lying around the house. Before you leave, be sure to thank Albert, Aunt Agnes, and Uncle Harry for a very nice vacation. Even if your week hasn't been fun, thank them anyway.

After you've thanked them personally, there's still one more thing you have to do. You have to write a thank-you letter as soon as you get home (you can say hello to your mother and father, and unpack your suitcase first).

Dear aunt Agnes,
I hope Albert doesn't
have a kidney disease!
I had a really nice time
in Minneapolis and
I really didn't
mean to break

CHAPTER FIVE

THANK-YOU LETTERS

You've been home for two days now, and you still haven't written to Aunt Agnes or Albert. And your mother keeps nagging, "Sybil, did you write your letters yet?"

Your mother knows very well that you didn't write your letters yet, but she keeps asking anyway.

The thing is, you're not sure how to go about writing a thank-you letter.

To begin with, it might be a good idea to have a pen and some paper. It's best to save your shocking purple ink and orange stationery for close friends and relatives. But a pen that writes in blue or black ink, and a light-colored stationery such as white, yellow, or pale blue is right for everyone; especially people you don't know too well.

You should write in your very best handwriting so your letter will be easy to read. Pay attention to your spelling, but don't worry too much about it. More important than your spelling, handwriting, and the color of your ink and stationery is the feeling that goes into your letter—what you say and the way you say it.

Put the date in the upper right-hand corner, and write a nice, natural letter to Aunt Agnes.

April 15, 19—

Dear Aunt Agnes,

I've been home for 2 days now, and I still can't stop thinking about the wonderful visit I had with you.

It was so nice of you to take me shopping at Daytons and Donaldsons. I didn't know Minneapolis had such big department stores.

And it was nice of Uncle Henry to spend all that time with me. I didn't know Minnesota had so many lakes!

Thank you very much, and I think you make the best sunny-side up eggs ever!

Love,
Sybil

Now write a letter to Albert.

April 15

Dear Albert,

Marcia and Irma tell me how they wish I would stop talking about my trip to Minneapolis. But I can't help it. We sure did have a lot of fun together.

Remember when we set up a lemonade stand but nobody wanted to buy any because they thought the cups were dirty so we had to drink all of it ourselves?

I'm sorry about your kite. Is it still in the tree? I'll bring you another one when I come back to Minneapolis.

Love,
Sybil

(If you don't want to say *love* you can say *Your cousin, Sybil*.)

Envelopes

You can't expect Aunt Agnes to receive your letter if you just write, "Aunt Agnes, Minneapolis, Minnesota," on the envelope. You have to write her complete address:

87

Mrs. Agnes Macintosh
22 Avenue East
Minneapolis, Minn.
55404

For Albert you write:

Albert Macintosh
22 Avenue East
Minneapolis, Minn.
55404

You should also put your own address in the upper left-hand corner of the envelope (or on the back flap), and a stamp in the upper right-hand corner. Try not to put the stamp on upside down.

Thank-You Letters When You've Received A Gift

It's always a nice gesture to send a thank-you

letter whenever you receive a gift. It's especially important to write one if somebody sends a gift and you are unable to say thank you in person. Otherwise the sender will either think you didn't like the gift, or that it was lost in the mail.

Let's suppose your grandmother sent you five dollars for your birthday. If your grandmother was thoughtful enough to send you a present, you should be thoughtful enough to write her a thank-you letter. Besides, your mother will probably make you do it anyway. So you take your pen and write:

February 15

Dear Grandmom,
    Thank you for the present.
            Love,
            Sybil

A letter like this is easy to write, but it has no meaning. You made no mention of what the present was, and you didn't say a thing about it. You could just as easily have bought a card and filled in the blanks.

Dear_____,
    Thank you for the_____.
            From_____

So you tear up the letter and start over.

89

February 16

Dear Grandmother,
    Thanks for the money. I hope my mother doesn't make me put it in the bank.
        Love,
        Sybil

Tear up that letter too. You can do better.

February 17,

Dear Grandmom,
    You couldn't have sent a more perfect gift for my birthday. I'm going to use the money to buy a pair of roller skates — the kind with rubber on the wheels.
    My friend Marcia promised to teach me how to skate this spring. And now that I can buy my own skates I won't have to borrow hers.
    Thank you for never forgetting my birthday.
        Love,
        Sybil

Now let's suppose you have to write a thank-you letter to someone you don't know too well. You don't know what to say, and you don't want to close the letter with *Love, Sybil*. What do you do?

Remember Mrs. Higgenbottom? She sent you a present for your birthday because she thought you were so charming and polite that day she met you.

The present is a beautiful blue sweater that matches your eyes. It's soft and cuddly, and fits you perfectly. You just love the sweater and can hardly wait to wear it.

This should be an easy letter to write because you liked the sweater so much. Say what you feel.

February 16

Dear Mrs. Higgenbottom,

Thank you for the beautiful blue sweater. It matches my eyes. It's soft and cuddly and fits me perfectly.

I just love the sweater and can hardly wait to wear it.

Thank you for thinking of me.

Sincerely yours,
Sybil

But suppose Mrs. Higgenbottom sent you a sweater that you absolutely hate?

Dear Mrs. Higgenbottom,
I don't thank you for
that wretchy gross ughly
hideous sweater (if thats
what its supposed to be)
Disgustedly yours,
Sybil

It's a combination of your least favorite colors
—pea green, murky brown and dusty gray. It's too
big and it itches. Marcia likes the sweater but your
mother won't let you give it to her. You don't know
where Mrs. Higgenbottom bought that ugly thing
so you can't even return it. What do you do in a
case like this?

You know what you would LIKE to write.

> February 19
>
> Dear Mrs. Higgenbottom,
>   No thank you for the
> sweater. It's a combination of
> my least favorite colors. It's
> too big and it itches. Please tell
> me where you bought that ugly
> thing so I can return it.
>   Yours truly,
>   Sybil

But please don't write a letter like that. It
wouldn't be polite. Mrs. Higgenbottom meant well.
You and she just have different tastes in sweaters.
Besides, a note like that would hurt her feelings,
and you wouldn't want to do that . . . ever.

You don't have to become a liar and tell Mrs.
Higgenbottom how much you like her present, but
you could say something like:

94

> *February 20.*
>
> Dear Mrs. Higgenbottom,
>
> Thank you for the sweater. It was very thoughtful of you to send it to me for my birthday. When my friend Marcia saw the sweater she couldn't stop telling me how much she liked it.
>
> There were 14 girls at my party and I got 4 comb and brush sets. But yours was the only sweater.
>
> Very truly yours,
> Sybil

More About Letters

It's always very nice to send letters or cards to people on their birthdays or when they're sick.

If you mail a letter you wrote when you were angry with someone, you might be sorry afterwards. So go ahead and write the letter—keep it until you cool off—then tear it up.

95

CHAPTER SIX

GROOMING

It's hard enough to wake up in time for school without having to worry about the way you look. But your mother is always nagging you about all kinds of little things.

"Sybil, brush your teeth."

You have all sorts of reasons why you don't brush your teeth too often:

1. You don't want to wear away your enamel.
2. You're too weak to squeeze the tube.
3. Toothpaste gets into the rivers and causes pollution.

These are three very good excuses, but you don't believe any of them. Deep down you know

97

the real reason. You're lazy! It's just too much trouble to brush your teeth, and you can think of better things to do with your time. But your mother keeps on nagging and drops all kinds of little hints. Like she'll say, "Sybil, when was the last time you saw a TV commercial promising brown teeth?"

So you look at your teeth in the mirror to see if your mother is trying to tell you something. She is. Your teeth are brown.

You begin to wonder if maybe it's time to get into the habit of brushing more often so you can get rid of the stain before it becomes permanent.

Two handy little items to have if you're planning on brushing your teeth are a toothbrush and a tube of toothpaste. Toothpaste comes in all sorts of colors and flavors, and it might be fun to experiment with different kinds.

The most important times to brush your teeth are in the morning when you wake up, after meals, and at night before you go to sleep. And there's no rule saying you can't brush during the day once in a while; especially if you've eaten something gooey like a taffy apple. And especially if you wear braces —in which case you shouldn't have had that taffy apple to begin with.

You brush the way your teeth grow—up and down. Not sideways. Brush real good and don't swallow the toothpaste. Rinse your mouth with cold water and rinse your toothbrush too. And if you use an electric toothbrush, don't forget to turn it off.

If a piece of food gets stuck in your teeth, and brushing doesn't help, try a piece of dental floss. It's much better than poking around with tooth-picks.

Before long, brushing your teeth will become a habit you won't want to break. And you will soon be flashing the same bright, white smile you see in the magazine ads.

"Sybil, wash your face."

Now how does your mother know you didn't wash your face? When you woke up in the morning you took a look in the mirror and saw that all the dirt from the day before was gone. It probably rubbed off on your pillow, you've decided. But what you don't understand is how your mother knows you didn't *wash* it off.

You take another look and you think you see the answer. Your face is asleep. Your eyes are open, but your face is still sleeping. You splash some cold water on your cheeks, dab a little around your eyes, and behold. The sleepy look is gone.

Well, maybe your face isn't sleeping anymore, but it isn't clean either. And if you want to have a pretty face, you have to start with a clean face.

A clean face means keeping dirty fingers away from it. A clean face means washing it—twice a day—when you wake up and before you go to sleep.

... AND HER EXQUISITE FEATURES WOULD BE SCARRED FOREVER, BY THE POISON FOAM WHICH THE SLAVERING MONSTER DASHED INTO HER PROUDLY MOCKING FACE! SHE RECOILED VIOLENTLY ...

And of course, during the day whenever it gets dirty.

Before you begin washing, you might want to tie your hair back so it won't get in the way. Start with clean hands, lukewarm water and plenty of soap. Work up a good lather in your hands and wash your face in circular motions. Don't cheat and skip the places you think no one will notice. Wash all over—around your hairline, behind your ears, and under your chin. And don't forget your neck. When you're finished washing, rinse off every bit of soap and pat your face dry with a soft, clean towel. Don't rub.

If you wash your face like this from now on, you'll not only look clean and wide awake, but you'll be starting yourself on the road to a clear, healthy-looking complexion.

"Sybil, you look like you could use a bath."

As far as you're concerned, the perfect time to take a bath (or shower) is never. The mornings are so short, you barely have enough time to go to the bathroom. And besides, you can't take a bath and run right out. You'll get pneumonia.

As for the evenings—well, there's all that homework to do. And baths keep you awake. How will you ever get your full twelve hours of sleep?

Baths are just not for you, you've decided. They make you feel so . . . wet.

You've done a very good job of talking yourself out of keeping clean. But have you noticed lately that nobody wants to sit next to you? Even Marcia and Irma kind of move away whenever you come near. So you rush home and splash your mother's expensive French perfume all over yourself so you'll smell nice. But Marcia and Irma keep on moving.

The truth is, you don't need perfume. You need a bath. All the expensive perfumes in the world will not cover up what's going on underneath. They'll never take the place of soap and water.

And who knows? Maybe if you try a few baths, you might even find that you like them. Baths do more than keep you clean. They relax you and soften your skin. And they're fun too—especially bubble baths. And if you're in a hurry, showers are great.

After your bath, when you're all dry, you can

dust yourself with some nice-smelling dusting powder, and just sit around feeling good.

You'll probably get to like baths so much, you might even want to take one every day. And Marcia and Irma will be sitting close to you again.

"Sybil, do something about your hair."

Now what does your mother mean by that? Your hair looks all right to you. And you already did something about it. When you woke up you pulled your hair away from your face, stuck a few bobby pins in all the right places, and now you can see again. So what else do you have to do?

Probably a whole lot. Otherwise you might be surprised to find out that an entire family of black widow spiders made a nest in your hair.

Shampooing Your Hair

Let's start off with a clean head. To have a clean head you have to shampoo your hair. And you should do it at least once a week.

You can wash your hair in the sink or under the faucet in the bathtub. An inexpensive rubber hose attachment is great for this. But you might find it easiest to wash it in the shower. If you don't like showers much, close your eyes and pretend you're outside washing your hair in the rain.

No matter where you do your shampooing, brush your hair real good first. Brushing loosens the dirt and takes out all those tangles you've collected.

... AS THE GENTLE WARM SPRING RAINS WASHED OVER THE EXQUISITE BUT BROKEN BODY OF THE LOVELY SPY WHO HAD BEEN LEFT UPON THE DESERTED MOOR, THE MONSTER MISTAKENLY BELIEVING HER TO BE DEAD, SHE SMILED INWARDLY, KNOWING THAT HER CLEVER RUSE HAD SUCCEEDED AND THAT HER.....

Now for the shampoo. If you always manage to get soap in your eyes, try a gentle no-sting baby shampoo. You wet your hair, put a small amount of shampoo in the palm of your hand, rub it into your hair and massage your scalp briskly all over. (Step away from the spray before you put the shampoo in your hair or it'll get washed away.)

Sometimes you don't get a good soaping the first time, so rinse and shampoo it again. When you think you've done a good job of shampooing, you have to do a good job of rinsing. Otherwise your hair will look even dirtier than it did before the shampoo. It'll be dull and sticky. You can sometimes tell if all the soap is out when your hair starts to squeak as you rub it. But the best way is to rinse it so thoroughly that there couldn't possibly be any soap left, and then—rinse it once more. Remember to comb your hair (with a clean comb) before it dries. Otherwise it'll dry with tangles and you'll have a hard time combing it later. And if you comb your hair while it's still wet, you can style your hair the way you'd like it to look when its's dry. But never go to bed with a wet head, because you might be shocked by the style you wake up with.

If you do end up with a mass of tangles, don't get angry and pull and tear at your hair with a comb. Gently separate the hair with a brush.

Brushing Your Hair

You've heard a lot about how you're supposed to brush your hair with 100 strokes every night before you go to sleep. You're sure your arm will fall off if you ever did that, so you figure you'll just skip the brushing.

Brushing is very good for your hair. It keeps your hair clean and shiny, and it does good things for your scalp too. So even if you can't manage 100 strokes every night, how about seventy-five . . . or fifty . . . or twenty-five? Ten maybe?

A good way to brush your hair and to help the circulation of your blood is to bend your head down and start brushing from the nape of the neck forward. Then, start at the forehead and brush back. When you think you've done enough brushing, comb or brush your hair back into place.

And in the morning, before you walk out of the house, be sure to brush or comb your hair. Even if you've had your bath and shampoo, you'll still look a mess if your hair isn't combed.

Wearing The Right Hair Style

How should you wear your hair?

1. The way Marcia wears her hair?
2. The way your mother wears her hair?
3. The way Mayor Willoughby wears his hair?
4. The way you look best?

If you chose number four you're correct. The style that's right for someone else may not be right for you.

Take Irma for instance. Irma wears bangs and she looks great. You would love to wear bangs too, except when you wear bangs you look like a sheep dog.

Marcia parts her hair in the middle. You like the way she looks with the part in the middle. You tried it once but a middle part makes your

face look like it's cut in half. So you go back to wearing your hair parted on the side. You look nice
that way.

And for all you know, Irma wishes she could
wear a side part instead of bangs, and Marcia wishes
she could part her hair on the side instead of in
the middle.

It might be fun to try different hair styles to
see which ones are best for you.

Don't use rubber bands if you wear your hair
in a pony tail. Rubber bands pull your hair and
split the ends. You can buy bands made especially
for pony tails at the dime store.

106

"Sybil, look at those nails."

So you look at your fingernails and you can't
see anything wrong with them. They're a little
dirty maybe, but other than that they're not so bad.
In fact, seven of them look pretty good to you.
You've taken great pains to grow them long, and
for days you've carefully filed them sharp and
pointy. You are now the proud owner of seven
deadly daggers to use as weapons in case you have
another fight with Albert.

Extra long, sharp nails can be dangerous. Not
only for Albert, but for you too. And besides that
they don't look very pretty—especially when they're
dirty.

Of course you can always cover up the dirt by
polishing your nails a blood red. But then you
would have seven blood-red deadly daggers.

Extra long, sharp nails are also bad for playing
piano. You can't curve your fingers. And you know
Miss Muldoon is forever telling you to curve your
fingers. If you curve your fingers with long nails,
they make a clicking sound on the keys. What you
need is a nail clipper.

Remember that pretty fingers start with clean
hands. So before you ever use the clipper, wash
your hands with plenty of soap and water.

With the clipper, cut off those extra long nails.
But be careful not to cut them too short. Stubby
looking nails aren't very attractive either. Then
take your emery board (the one you used to make

107

your daggers), and file your nails to a nice oval shape. Keep your nails clean, and your hands will always be pretty to look at.

And don't forget to cut your toenails.

"Sybil, you look like you just stepped out of the clothes hamper."

How did your mother guess? Actually, you didn't come out of the hamper, but your dress did.

There was this blue dress you wanted to wear, and while you were hunting for it in the closet, you remembered that it was in the clothes hamper. You wore the dress about five days ago, and when you spilled catsup all over the front of it you threw it in the hamper. (You know better than to hang up dirty clothes in the closet.)

You were really in the mood to wear that dress today, so you pulled it out of the hamper, sort of washed off the catsup and smoothed out a few wrinkles. Does your mother appreciate the effort? No! She tells you the dress is dirty, and you shouldn't wear dirty clothes.

Deep down you know your mother is right. Your blue dress, no matter how pretty it is, will look ugly if it's dirty. So you go back to your room and change.

Clothes Should Fit Neatly

You throw on a clean skirt and blouse and are all ready for a little breakfast before you dash off to school. But your mother still isn't satisfied. She says you look like a mess.

"I'm clean!" you yell. And she tells you to take a good look at yourself in the mirror.

When you do, you see that your blouse is hanging out of your skirt, your collar is turned under, you've buttoned wrong, and your skirt is held together with safety pins. Maybe you do look a little messy—especially around the safety pins. But there's no time to sew buttons on your skirt, so you go back to your room to change—again.

Clothes Should Not Be Cluttered With Unnecessary Decorations

You are all set to cry, "I have nothing to wear," when you remember the blouse and jumper your mother bought you last year. The outfit was too big for you then, and you couldn't return it because it was bought on sale. But you're hoping you've grown into it by now, so you hurry up and try it on.

The blouse is a turtleneck pullover with a short zipper in the back. You put it on and even remember to zip the zipper. It fits perfectly and you have no buttons to worry about. Next you try on the jumper. It's just the right length. You're sure your mother will be pleased.

But is she? No! She wants to know why you're walking around with all those tags hanging on your clothes.

Upon close examination you find that there

are three of them. The first tag, which is sticking out of the armpit, shows that your new outfit was reduced from $9.95 to $8.50. You figure it's nobody's business how much it costs, so you remove the tag. The second tag attached to a pocket on your jumper says, "Wash in Woolite," and the third one, hanging from the zipper on your blouse says, "Permanent Press" and "Made in Philadelphia."

You get rid of those tags, too, and now that you're finally ready to leave for school, you find that you've missed the school bus and have to walk.

To avoid getting into further situations of this sort, you should:

1. Decide what you want to wear the night before.
2. Check to see if it's clean.
3. Check to see if it fits.
4. Check to see that all buttons are sewn on.
5. Stay home from school.

That was a tricky little quiz. The last answer was the wrong one. All the others were right.

Wearing The Right Colors and Styles

Irma told you that she likes your turtleneck blouse. She says you look great in turtlenecks, and she wishes she could wear them too; except that turtlenecks make her look like a real turtle.

Irma is smart enough to recognize an important truth—clothes that look good on one person might not look good on somebody else. The same is true of colors.

Marcia, for instance, wears brown and beige very well. Brown and beige make you look sick. You are a blue person. Of course this doesn't mean you have to wear blue turtlenecks for the rest of your life. But it's a good idea to get to know the styles and colors that are best for you.

Clothes Should Fit The Occasion

Your mother and father have been invited to a fancy dinner party. You were invited too. Actually, you would rather stay home, but your mother and father are making you go.

So you throw on a pair of sneakers and the old pair of jeans you wore last Tuesday when you were learning how to roller skate. The knee patches are full of holes made from falling down a lot, and you can even see a little dried blood around the edges. But these jeans are still your favorite. You feel so comfortable in them.

Do your parents understand? No! They tell you to take off those old rags and put on your party dress and party shoes so you'll look like a lady.

You are not a lady and you can't understand why you have to look like one. But you change anyway.

And it's good that you do. If people think enough of you to invite you to a dinner party, and

111

try to make you special by putting out flowers and their best linens and dishes, wouldn't it be nice of you to dress your best and show them that they're special too?

Save your jeans for the time you're invited to a backyard barbeque, or for the next time you go roller skating.

"Sybil, your room looks like it was hit by a tornado."

Remember when you were looking in the closet and had a hard time finding something to wear? That's because you looked in the wrong place. You hardly ever keep your things in the

closet anymore. Mostly your clothes can be found lying on the bed, lying on the floor, lying on top of your dresser, hanging on the doorknobs, and hanging over chairs.

Not only does your room look a mess, but so do your clothes. Ordinarily, none of this would bother you. But your mother says she's tired of having to shut the door to your room every time company comes over, and that you can't go out to play with Marcia until you hang up all your clothes.

You figure it'll be midnight by the time you get everything back in the closet, and most of your clothes are all wrinkled up anyway. So you just dump the whole heap in the hamper.

113

You won't ever have a problem like this if you remember to put away each item of clothing as soon as you're finished wearing it. Dirty things should be put in the hamper and clean clothes should be hung up in the closet or put back in the drawers.

If you don't collect any more piles of clothes, you will have more time to play with Marcia . . . or Irma . . . or Bruce.

"Sybil, your shoes are dirty."

Remember that little spat you had with Marcia? She said you had dirty shoes, and you said she had big feet, and she cried and you had to apologize.

Well, the whole thing never would have happened if your shoes were clean.

Shoes are an important part of your clothing. So while you're picking out your clothes for the next day, check to see if your shoes need cleaning. Some shoes have to be polished and other shoes can be cleaned by wiping them with a damp cloth. If your heels are rundown, be sure to get new ones put on.

Check your shoelaces (if you wear shoelaces), and if they look like Shredded Wheat, it's time to get new ones. Keep them tied too, so you won't walk out of your shoes, or trip and fall on your face.

"Sybil, did you change your underwear?"

Change your underwear? What for? Nobody

ever sees your underwear, so why change?

Even though people can't see your underwear, they have a way of knowing when you're in need of a change; just like they have a way of knowing when you need a bath. Clean clothes over dirty underwear doesn't make a whole lot of sense. So right along with your daily bath, you should treat yourself to a change of underwear and socks.

If you always seem to run short of clean underwear and socks, maybe it's because you keep putting the dirty ones back in the drawer. Check your drawers once in a while. You might find some interesting things going on in there—even some things that aren't yours.

Never lend or borrow—

1. Unwashed underwear
2. Toothbrushes
3. Gum that's been chewed
4. Combs and brushes

YOUR POSTURE

"Sybil, stand up straight and tall like a model."

Your mother keeps telling you to stand up straight and tall like a model, and you don't even want to be a model. But the other day you caught a glimpse of yourself in a store window reflection, and you looked like a camel. You're a bit on the tall side and you figured you would look shorter if you slouched a little. But all the time you thought you

were looking shorter you were really looking like a camel.

After you thought about looking like a camel, you decided you'd rather look like a model. So now you keep your shoulders back, your back straight and your head erect. Your clothes seem to fit better and you look prettier too.

You Need Good Posture When You Sit

When Miss Muldoon isn't telling you to curve your fingers, she's telling you to sit up straight. She says pianists have to sit properly in order to play well.

Miss Muldoon is a fine one to talk. She's not all that perfect either. Miss Muldoon has dandruff. You see it on her shoulders all the time and you get the urge to brush it off.

You could tell her a thing or two about grooming, but you don't. She's older than you and you are still showing her some respect. So you forget about her dandruff and concentrate on sitting up straight.

You should sit up straight all the time; even when you're not playing the piano. You should sit well back in your chair; not slumped over the edge. Your back should be straight and your hands should be in a comfortable position in your lap or on the arms of the chair (unless you are playing piano). Sitting with your knees spread apart doesn't look very pretty, so you cross your legs or ankles gracefully (unless you are playing the piano and have to use the pedals).

AVOIDING UGLY HABITS

There are some habits that are good to get into. Like the habits of brushing your teeth and washing your face and taking a bath and all those others that were mentioned before. But there are

117

other habits that are good to get *out* of. And sometimes it's harder to get *out* of a habit than it is to get *into* one.

You've picked up quite a few juicy little habits lately. They involve picking, biting, scratching, and grinding, and they're driving your mother and father crazy. You don't do all these things at the same time, so you can't understand why they get so excited. Your habits come and go, one at a time. And one at a time your mother and father complain about them.

Last week for instance, you were onto scabs. You have scads of scabs—on your elbows and on your knees. And you just love to pick them off. Sometimes you get so involved in your picking that you don't even realize you're doing it. But your father has a way of reminding you. "Sybil, stop that picking! It looks terrible and you'll get an infection."

Well, maybe he's right. So you try picking something else—like your nose, or maybe in between your teeth. But your father yells, "Stop it!" again. He says that picking—any kind of picking— just doesn't look nice.

And to top it off, even your orthodontist (if you go to an orthodontist) is on your back. Whenever you pick at your braces he tells you to stop tampering with your appliances (that's what he calls them).

So this week you've given up scabs (there aren't too many left anyway), noses, teeth and braces, and you've started on nails. You just love to nibble on your fingers. You figure that by biting your nails you are accomplishing two things at the same time. You're keeping your mouth busy and you're giving yourself a manicure. But what do you do with them once you've bitten them off? You can't swallow them, so you just sort of spit them out.

Your mother says, "Sybil, it's disgusting!"

"What's disgusting?" you ask.

"The way you bite your nails and the way you spit them out. And your fingers—just look at them!"

So you look at your fingers and think that maybe you'll have to start wearing mittens from now on. Your fingers look awful. You hardly have any nails left. And without nails how will you ever scratch your head?

Scratching is another habit you've picked up along the way. You just love to sit and scratch your head; especially when you're deep in concentration. Scratching helps you think. But it makes your father nervous. He tells you to stop it and go do something. So you figure you'll grind your teeth for a while. But even that upsets him.

Now if all these little habits of yours annoy your own parents, just imagine what they do to other people who have to look at you. And just think of how you feel when you see somebody else picking and biting and scratching and grinding the way you do. It's enough to make your skin crawl. It should be enough to make you stop.

Chewing Gum

You might not think that chewing gum has anything to do with appearance, but it does.

Imagine yourself being beautifully dressed, standing straight and tall like a model, with your long, shiny brown hair neatly parted on the side.

You are sure that everyone notices you—and they do; but it's not your clothes they notice, or your posture or your hair. They are noticing your bubble gum and the way it's hanging halfway out of your mouth as you chew.

You can chew any way you want to—when you're alone and there's nobody around to watch. You can chew five pieces of bubble gum at one time, crack it, and blow bubbles bigger than your face. You can even stretch it and use it as a jump rope. *But* when you chew gum in public, you should chew in such a way that it doesn't look like you're chewing—slowly and quietly with your mouth closed.

After all the flavor is gone, don't just spit out your gum on the sidewalk or leave it sitting in a drinking fountain somewhere. Not only is that littering, but think of how disgusting it is to step in someone's gum or to see a wad of it staring up at you from a drinking fountain. So wrap it up in a piece of paper, and find a waste basket to throw it in.

Or better yet, ask yourself if you and your teeth really need to chew gum in the first place.

GETTING ENOUGH EXERCISE

Lately you've noticed that Irma is putting on a little extra weight. She does a lot of eating and a lot of sitting. She's also doing a lot of spreading. So now her mother is after her to do some exercises and go on a diet.

You feel lucky that you're not fat. You'd hate to have to give up eating and do a lot of strenuous exercises.

First of all, everybody needs exercise. Not just fat people. Daily exercise keeps your body in good shape and improves your health. It makes you feel better too. And another thing, not all exercises are strenuous. Some of them—the very best of them—are also the most fun to do. You are probably doing a few exercises without even realizing it. Some exercises that don't seem like exercises are:

1. walking
2. running
3. bike riding
4. skating
5. swimming
6. jumping rope
7. dancing

So if you can have fun and keep in good shape at the same time, why sit around all day? Get out and do things. Keep active. And instead of asking your father to drive you around all over the place—

like down the block and around the corner—try walking for a change. Keep on taking those walks to Woolworth's too. And ask Irma to go with you.

EATING THE RIGHT KIND OF FOOD

While Irma has been wondering why she's getting so fat, Marcia has been wondering why she's getting so many cavities.

You suggest that maybe they've been eating too many coconut-covered marshmallows and cashews and hot fudge sundaes. But Marcia says there's no such thing as too many coconut-covered marshmallows and cashews and hot fudge sundaes. "Besides," she says, "you eat all those things too. How come you don't have any cavities and you're not getting fat?"

You tell Marcia that you've just been lucky so far. And then you begin to wonder how long your luck will hold out. You don't want teeth like Marcia's or a body like Irma's. And you don't want to take the chance of getting pimples either. You've been looking pretty good lately, and you'd like to stay that way.

Your appearance not only depends on what you do to the outside of you, but also on what you do for your insides.

So instead of filling up on all those snacks with Marcia and Irma, you should start to eat more of the good foods that are around: fruits (especially those yummy summertime fruits), and vegetables, and milk and juices. The right food along with plenty of rest and exercise will keep everything about you in perfect shape.

CONCLUSION

You and Marcia are outside playing a game of jacks. A mail truck pulls up in front of your house and the mailman comes out and hands you a package. You're all excited because someone has sent you a present. You know it's for you because it has your name, *Sybil Macintosh,* right on the label.

The present is a book from your Aunt Mildred who lives in Portland. And of all things, it's a book on manners and grooming. It seems that Aunt Mildred doesn't know about the new you. She remembers you from the olden days when you were hiding in the closet. It was nice of your aunt to send you the book, but you really won't be needing it. When it comes to manners and grooming, you're an expert. You're charming and polite and thoughtful and nice to be with. And you've noticed that there have been all kinds of changes lately.

Your mother says *may I* before she turns off the TV in the middle of your favorite program, and she introduces you to everyone she meets. She holds her head high when she says, "This is my daughter Sybil."

Your father, who no longer yells at you at the dinner table, now talks of interesting things—like sending you to visit a cousin in Scarborough, Ontario—all because your manners are so terrific.

Marcia and Irma are more polite and nicer to be with too. Your thoughtful ways seems to be spreading. Who knows how far they'll reach or who they'll touch.

Do you know what? You've come a long way, Sybil Macintosh!

Charlotte Herman was sorely tempted to be rude to the first person she met after she finished writing about manners . . . but settled instead on setting the dinner table backwards while her family stood agog.

Mrs. Herman is also the author of the Lead-Off Book, *Stringbean,* and a fiction story for girls, *The Three of Us.* She lives with her well-groomed husband, four polite children, and ill-mannered beagle pup, Humphrey, in Lincolnwood, Illinois.

Trina Schart Hyman is a wondrously talented artist who has illustrated many books for children. She also works as art director for the new children's magazine, *Cricket.* Ms. Hyman and her daughter Katrin live on a farm in New Hampshire.